D1626338

CHICHESTER
THEN & NOW
IN COLOUR

PHILIP MACDOUGALL

First published in 2012

The History Press
The Mill, Brimscombe Port
Stroud, Gloucestershire, GL5 2QG
www.thehistorypress.co.uk

© Philip MacDougall, 2012

The right of Philip MacDougall to be identified as the Author
of this work has been asserted in accordance with the
Copyrights, Designs and Patents Act 1988.

British Library Cataloguing in Publication Data.
A catalogue record for this book is available from the British Library.

ISBN 978 0 7524 7142 6

Typesetting and origination by The History Press
Printed in India.

CONTENTS

ACKNOWLEDGEMENTS

The author would like to thank the following for photographs used in this book: the late Dave Turner (pages 40, 59 and 84); Chichester District Museum (pages 24, 39, 53, 76 and 78); Judith O'Sullivan (page 22); the late Alan Williams (page 51); Shippam's Ltd (page 72); and Portsmouth Water (page 93).

ABOUT THE AUTHOR

Since settling in Chichester, Philip has written extensively on the history of the area, having now written five books that focus entirely on the city or its immediate surroundings. A further book, *If War Should Come*, looks at a number of towns and cities along the south coast, including Chichester, and considers how prepared they were for the long-predicted war that broke out in September 1939. His interest in Chichester does not extend just to history but also to the future of the city, with Philip actively involved in a number of issues to improve the nature of the overall environment.

East Street, Chichester, in 1903.

INTRODUCTION

Chichester is a city in the midst of a crisis. How does it meet the needs of a rapidly changing world while retaining both its character and age-old charm? The threat now being faced is threefold: that of the city and its immediate area being overwhelmed by housing and other developments, the constant demand for more roads, and several of the more recent planning consents given for questionable flagship developments.

Over 1,000 new homes are in the pipeline for construction within the Chichester city area, the majority of which are to be built on the former sites of the Graylingwell Hospital (750 new homes) and Roussillon Barracks (252 new homes). In addition, recent housing projects have been completed alongside the canal basin and Eastgate Square, and further housing has been developed on the south side of land formerly belonging to the girls' high school. On top of all this, more planning requests are likely to emerge over the next few years. While the majority of houses to be built may have much to be commended (those at Graylingwell and the Barracks are designed to achieve a minimum carbon emission) it seems unlikely that each new resident will fail to plant some kind of carbon footprint. In other words, such a vast number of new permanent residents, more in number than previously have ever arrived in Chichester in such a short space of time, will result (not least) in several hundred more cars on roads already at full stretch.

So why not simply build more roads? In part, because new roads simply generate more cars while doing much to destroy the character of the area through which they pass. Instead, the role of public transport, through the use of imaginative solutions, needs to be looked at more carefully. Unfortunately, this is not the direction being taken. Both the County Council and Chichester District Council have failed to see the big picture. With regard to the former, rather than increasing bus subsidies they have had the temerity to reduce them – so forcing hundreds more onto the roads. Similarly, instead of directing money to build a long-promised bus-rail interchange, the District Council have plumped for a new museum building, much criticised locally for its architectural design.

And this, quite neatly, brings us to the third threat that is facing Chichester, that of approval being given to poorly designed flagship developments that, if continued, will turn the city into a featureless concrete jungle. This trend began with the former Telephone Exchange in Chapel Street, driven forward by the extension to Pallant House and firmly sealed by the new museum building. Where will it end? Possibly with Chichester becoming a clone town, similar in every respect to a myriad of other featureless UK cities that have had the essence of their former selves ripped out and replaced.

Of course, actions could be taken to generally improve the nature and character of the city. Long-term planning of the architectural development of the city would be valuable, recognising the city is inherently Georgian in both style and ethos. Also positive would be the District Council not only in encouraging more businesses but establishing more of its own facilities in this area including, as an example, an annex to the Westgate Leisure Centre in an existing retail unit. Another important improvement would be that of making part of the area within the city walls a car-free area, while in residential streets the default speed limit might be reduced to 20mph, this last currently under serious discussion. Both moves, if carried out, and there is much support within the city, would allow residents to win back the roads and allow the Georgian architecture of the city to be better appreciated.

THE CATHEDRAL

IF THE CITY of Chichester is approached from the south-west, it is still possible to glimpse a not too dissimilar view of the cathedral as it appears in this eighteenth-century print. In the foreground were once to be seen Westgate fields, which were used for the grazing of cattle and remained a familiar sight well into the twentieth century. Indeed, the open fields running right up to the city walls remained until 1966 and completion of the then controversial Avenue de Chartres. Remaining with the earlier view and looking into the area bounded by the medieval wall, Westgate House (now Edes House), the tall building on the left, is to be glimpsed, while the north-west tower of the cathedral still awaits repair following a collapse that had occurred in 1630.

THE MODERN-DAY view, taken from the Bishop's Palace Gardens, in editing out the Avenue de Chartres, proves that areas of tranquillity and rustic charm are still to be found within the very depths of the city. Indeed, the Bishop's Palace Gardens are one of the best kept secrets of the area, approached through a footpath that leads away from the palace and cathedral. With a number of gardeners employed upon its upkeep, it is best seen during the summer when it is a riot of colour. The decision to build the road now named Avenue de Chartres followed a ten-year period of concentrated opposition to the project and the forcing of four public enquiries. In turn, of course, the completion of the new road permitted the partial pedestrianisation of the inner-wall shopping areas.

THE CATHEDRAL NAVE

CONSTRUCTION OF CHICHESTER Cathedral began in 1076, with this, the original Norman cathedral, completed and dedicated to the Holy Trinity in 1108. The appearance of that earlier building – the cathedral having seen many changes, additions and improvements since that date – can be best appreciated by an examination of the nave where the four eastern-most bays date to the early eleventh century. Such an appreciation is particularly enhanced by the nineteenth-century print viewed opposite, which has the advantage of showing the cathedral in an earlier, uncluttered state. As for the lack of pews, this results from most religious services at that time being held in the choir.

IN CONTRAST, THE modern-day view not only shows the addition of central hanging lights but also seating, which is a result of more use now being made of the nave. However, its elegance and beauty is still there to be appreciated – a fine example of medieval architecture in all its splendour. Elsewhere in the modern-day cathedral a number of pieces of late twentieth-century modern art are to be found, including a tapestry by John Piper, a painting by Graham Sutherland and a window by Marc Chagall.

THE SPIRE THAT DISAPPEARED

FOLLOWING A VIOLENT overnight storm in February 1861, the medieval tower and spire of the cathedral collapsed. While a degree of uncertainty existed as to the actual cause, fingers pointed at ongoing remedial work designed to strengthen the building following discovery of huge fissures in the supporting piers of the central tower. Although these were of long duration, having lain behind a large screen known as the Arundel Screen, then being removed, the mortar poured into the fissures had possibly failed to bond, helping undermine the existing structure. A further factor may have been the removal of the screen that was providing bracing on one side. A subsequent restoration, placed in the hands of Gilbert Scott, resulted in a replica central tower and spire that differed in being 8ft taller than the original. The contemporary illustration shows the crowning of the spire that took place on 28 June 1866.

THE PRESENT-DAY tower is viewed from a not dissimilar angle and also shows that, through the use of lighting, it is an important feature of the city at night. An obvious city landmark, the tower and spire of the cathedral are clearly visible from a number of the villages that surround the city. In

more recent years, the tower has become a nesting site for a pair of peregrine falcons during the summer months, with some thirty chicks having been raised since 2001. An additional attraction for the city, visitors are encouraged to view the nest from an information site situated within the grounds of the cathedral tea rooms. The scaffolding to be seen towards the top of the spire was, at the time of this photograph in November 2011, being used to install a cockerel weather-vane that had been gilded with Fairtrade and Fairmined gold. It was part of an ethically-minded collaboration between the cathedral, a local jeweller's and the Fairtrade Foundation. The first time that a Fairtrade and Fairmined piece of art has ever been publicly displayed, it also serves as a useful reminder of Chichester being a Fairtrade city as a result of the number of outlets selling Fairtrade products.

BISHOP'S PALACE

CONSTRUCTION OF THE Bishop's Palace began
sometime during the mid-twelfth century.
It was designed to serve as both a residence
for the bishop and as a seat for diocesan
administration. Little of that original building
remains other than the outside wall of the
kitchen, which displays two blocked windows
and a blocked door, all dating from the twelfth
century. It was a fire in 1187 which, in destroying
much of the palace, necessitated considerable
reconstruction, which was undertaken by Bishop
Seffrid II (1180-1204). Of the original Bishop's
Palace building, the chapel, two-storey hall and
kitchen still remain. The chapel, which stands
immediately to the south-west of the cathedral,
diagonally opposite the south-west tower, clearly
dates to around 1200, although the windows are
of a later insertion of about 1320. The earlier

view dates to the summer of 1921 when the bishop for Chichester was Winfrid Oldfield Burrows, formerly Bishop of Truro.

THE PRESENT-DAY Bishop's Palace was, until very recently, the home of The Right Reverend Dr John Hind, who was appointed to Chichester in 2001. Having announced that was to retire at the end of April 2012, he is to be succeeded by the Rt Revd Dr Martin Warner. Chichester is one of the oldest dioceses in the country, with the appointee often having the right to sit in the House of Lords. A significant twentieth-century resident of the palace was George Bell, Bishop of Chichester from 1929 to 1958. A forward-looking member of the Church, he fell foul of the establishment through his criticism of the use of indiscriminate carpet bombing of cities as carried out by the Allies during the Second World War. It is generally considered that this led to his being twice overlooked when consideration was being given to appointing a new Archbishop of Canterbury. In 1939, with evacuees from south London arriving in the city, he gave over much of the palace to the support of their needs.

CANON GATE

THE PRECINCTS OF the cathedral are surrounded by an enclosing wall that was built during the Middle Ages to more completely separate the chapter and other members of the cathedral from the ordinary citizens of the town. Various entry points pierced the wall, including Canon Gate, which provided access from South Street. Within the precinct, and apart from the Bishop's Palace, are located the Deanery, cloisters, Palace Gardens and residences once given over to members of the Chapter and others attached to the cathedral.

VIEWED FROM ITS west side, the gate has undergone a number of alterations, including the reshaping of the arch over the pedestrian walkway and the widening of the original carriage entry. Today, Canon Gate continues to offer entry to the cathedral and into a tranquil world that contrasts sharply with the hustle and bustle of South Street. A closer examination of the structure reveals that the upper story has a niche between the two windows. The windows are modern and have trefoil heads and square labels, but the weather-worn niche is ancient with brackets carved as demi-angels holding a shield that apparently bore the sacred monogram 'I H S'. A similar arrangement is also to be noted on the east side of the gate.

VICARS' CLOSE

VICARS' CLOSE WAS probably first laid out in 1147 when Bishop Hilary obtained a confirmation of land previously granted to the cathedral authorities and located within the south-west quarter of the city. Here, and over a lengthy period of time, various houses were built, including lodgings for vicars, those appointed to stand in for non-residential canons and who also sang the daily services. The latter, who were frequently appointed from among the king's clerks, were often called away to fulfil other duties and therefore not available for their official church duties. Of note is the layout of thoroughfares in this

area: these run parallel to West Street and not in accordance with the axis of the cathedral, suggesting that they followed the course of the original grid pattern as laid down in Roman times.

AS THIS MODERN view opposite demonstrates, there is much more of medieval Chichester than the highly visible walls and cathedral, Vicar's Close being one of those many little surprises that the city has to offer. Remaining in the ownership of the Dean and Chapter of Chichester, these properties in Vicars' Close (with fully modernised interiors) are commercially let, a situation that has been ongoing since the seventeenth century.

CHAPEL STREET

CHAPEL STREET IS one of two streets that lead northward off West Street. At one time its entire length was lined by eighteenth- and early nineteenth-century houses, many of them deserving of preservation. On the left of the earlier picture is the front of the old independent chapel of red brick and diapered with metallic grey headers. The brick terraced houses on the opposite side show that even some of the smallest and humblest buildings in the city were once dignified by such additions as porticoes.

THE DEMOLITION OF many of the early terraced houses on the west side of Chapel Street saw their replacement by one of the ugliest structures ever to be built in the city. This was the Telephone Exchange, a hideous box-like structure that had nothing in common with the buildings it overshadowed and which led to a high profile but ultimately unsuccessful campaign (led by the then Archdeacon of Chichester, the Venerable Lancelot Mason) to oppose it getting planning consent. Perhaps even more disastrous is that in being constructed, the Telephone Exchange set off a certain trend, with a number of other structures that add little to the city following in its wake. Fortunately, further north along Chapel Street, a number of those early porticoed houses have been retained, while the Telephone Exchange has now been refaced by courtesy of Travelodge.

THE PREBENDAL SCHOOL

THE PREBENDAL SCHOOL, located in West Street, is an ancient scholastic institution that was established by Bishop Edward Story (1478-1503) at the end of the fifteenth century to improve the general educational standards in the area. In establishing the new foundation, Bishop Story laid down a series of regulations that covered its general organisation. Dated February 1498, these regulations required that masters were to be appointed from among priests who were 'well and sufficiently instructed in Grammar, and other Literature, and apt in teaching' while declaring that scholars were to arrive in the school by 5 a.m. for attending Morning Mass.

THE PREBENDAL SCHOOL, albeit with less extreme hours of attendance,

continues to perform its role as an educational establishment, being nowadays a co-educational day/boarding school for children aged three to thirteen years. The youngest children start in the Pre-Prep at Northgate House before progressing in their later years to the site of the original school that is situated next to the cathedral.

VICAR'S HALL AND UNDERCROFT

THE UNDERCROFT IS a medieval building that lies on the west side of South Street, fronting the cathedral precincts, while the Vicar's Hall (the subject of the earlier photograph) is the building above. Both sections of the buildings are medieval, not just the basement or undercroft that is reached by steps leading down from South Street. However, it is this part of the building that has the earliest construction date and was the undercroft to the Guildhall, an important building where the city merchants met. During the Middle Ages the merchants of the city of Chichester were united in a single organised body known as a guild. This was responsible for regulating all trading activities, with members of the guild having unfettered rights to buy and sell within the area of the walls. Underpinning these rights was a royal charter, with the authority of an earlier (but now lost) charter confirmed by one issued by King Stephen (1134-54). In later years this, the city's first Guildhall, was acquired by the cathedral authorities who, while retaining the undercroft, rebuilt the upper part of the building for use of the Vicars' Choral of the cathedral for dining and entertaining.

THE UNDERCROFT OR basement to the original Guildhall has served for many years as a well situated restaurant at the top end of South Street, and it is currently The Buttery but was formerly the Crypt Coffee House. The age of the building becomes immediately clear to anyone descending the steps that lead into the main dining area.

ST PETER THE LESS

ST PETER THE Less was one of a number of small churches that served the city, each of them having absurdly small parishes. For this reason, most have become redundant, although in the

case of St Peter the Less, its fate was more extreme and it was demolished in 1957 to make way for a new Co-op store. Standing in North Street, and originally constructed in the thirteenth century, it possessed at that time a nave and chancel. During the following century, however, it was provided with a south aisle and tower, making it the largest of Chichester's medieval churches.

NOWADAYS, THE FORMER site of St Peter the Less is difficult to discern as no remains of the church survived its demolition. Indeed, the only clue to the church having been there is that of the road that now runs through where the church stood: it is called St Peter's. As for the retail store which replaced the church, this is now trading as Lakeland.

ST MARY'S HOSPITAL

MOST PROBABLY FOUNDED in the twelfth century, St Mary's Hospital is a charitable institution that was established to support the needs of the poor. Situated in the north-east quadrant of the city with an entrance off St Martin's Square, it moved to its present site during the third quarter of the thirteenth century, which is when the infirmary, hall and chapel were built. In this eighteenth-century print, the hall is to be seen and has the general appearance of a tower-less church. It is aisled with flint walls and timber framing, and the walls were once breached by a series of tiny, single light windows, similar to one still in existence on the south side.

TODAY, THE HOSPITAL is under the auspices of the Dean and Chapter of Chichester Cathedral,
who act as the trustees of the hospital and its endowments. St Mary's still supports the needs
of the poor, providing residential accommodation that has seen numerous improvements and
changes over the passing centuries but especially during the twentieth century. However, the hall
itself remains externally little changed although internally the layout has seen the introduction
of several self-contained units. An important historical building, those interested in its history
are able to visit the site but only by appointment.

THE CROSS

BISHOP STORY (1478-1503), who founded the Prebendal School, was also responsible for Chichester's most iconic monument, that of the stone Market Cross that stands at the intersection of the city's four main streets. It replaced an earlier wooden cross that had been erected on the same site by Bishop Rede (1369-85). The new Market Cross was not only a much grander affair but had the specific purpose of helping the poor of the area gain a regular income. On market days, those traders who were too poor to pay the dues and fees levied by the City Corporation were permitted to trade under the shelter of the Cross without payment. During the late nineteenth and early twentieth centuries a police officer was always to be found at the Cross, making it easy to locate an officer of the law when needs required. The earlier view of the Cross shows it surrounded by scaffolding that had been erected in 1928 to assist in an extensive restoration programme that had been made necessary by its dilapidated state that had made it dangerous to passers-by. The scaffolding used was erected in such a fashion as to allow the continued use of the encircling roads to traffic as, at that time, there was no by-pass.

IN CONTRAST TO the early twentieth-century daytime view of the Cross is this evening view taken in late October 2011. As might be noted, the surrounding area is virtually deserted, the city not particularly famous for its nightlife.

COUNCIL HOUSE

A LATE NINETEENTH-CENTURY view of the Council House competes with a view of the same building taken on an autumn evening in 2011. The building was constructed between 1729 and 1733 to house the common council or ruling body of the city, replacing an earlier Council House that had also stood on North Street, with this latter building demolished. A feature of the new building was that of it having a council chamber, a simple room incorporated into the first floor. An addition to the building came about in 1783 when

an east wing to accommodate an Assembly Room was added, this designed by James Wyatt. Assembly rooms were an important feature of eighteenth-century fashionable life as it was here that 'society' gathered. Regular concerts were once held, an organ added to the room in 1791.

ALTHOUGH CHICHESTER NO longer has an all-powerful city council that oversees the complete running of local affairs, the city council still exists. Its present-day powers include that of having an influence on planning matters while having the right to raise and spend money for the benefit of those who live within the area of the city. In reality the equivalent of a parish council for the city, the city council owns, on behalf of the citizens, the Council House with its Assembly Room and is landlord of the Market House (the Butter Market) in North Street. The city council also oversees the twinning activities between Chichester and the French city of Chartres and the Italian city of Ravenna. It is these twinnings that have led to Avenue de Chartres and Via Ravenna being so named.

CORN EXCHANGE

THE CORN EXCHANGE, one of Chichester's most impressive buildings, was constructed between 1832 and 1833 as an enclosed area for farmers to bring samples of harvested corn that they were selling. These samples were then used to extract bids from dealers, with the most favourable being accepted. At the front of the building stand six iron colonnades, each weighing three tons. In later years, the Corn Exchange has undergone a number of changes, becoming a cinema at the beginning of the twentieth century and later, towards the end of that same century, a fast food outlet.

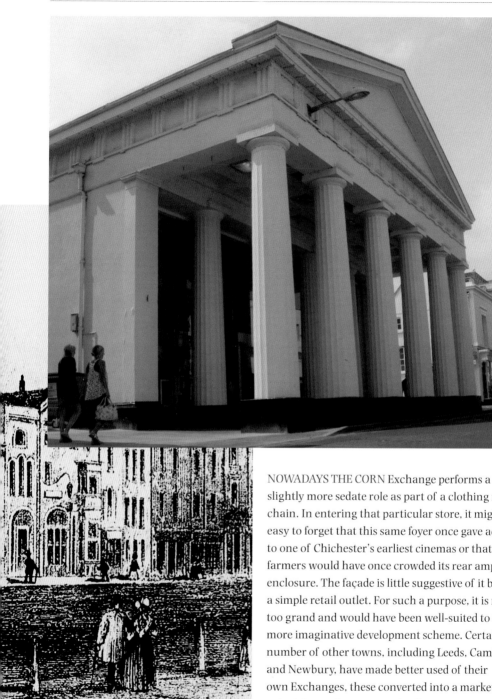

NOWADAYS THE CORN Exchange performs a slightly more sedate role as part of a clothing retail chain. In entering that particular store, it might be easy to forget that this same foyer once gave access to one of Chichester's earliest cinemas or that local farmers would have once crowded its rear ample enclosure. The façade is little suggestive of it being a simple retail outlet. For such a purpose, it is much too grand and would have been well-suited to a more imaginative development scheme. Certainly a number of other towns, including Leeds, Cambridge and Newbury, have made better used of their own Exchanges, these converted into a market, entertainment venue or art gallery.

THE BUTTERMARKET

ALTHOUGH ONLY A relatively short period separates these two photographs of the Buttermarket in North Street, the building has undergone extensive change. This resulted from a complete refurbishment carried out by the city council in 2010 with the building re-opened in early 2011. Originally built in 1807, and alternatively known as the Market House, it was originally designed by the famous London architect John Nash (1752-1835). Its purpose, then as now, was to provide room for enclosed trading and it was designed to replace the Market Cross. The top storey was not part of the original design, this being added in 1900.

THE REFURBISHMENT OF the Buttermarket has given the building a greater degree of spaciousness together with a much lighter and airier feel. Altogether it is a much more exciting building that welcomes its visitors and encourages them to stay. Furthermore, it is an impressive Georgian building that, by providing space for small retail outlets, helps Chichester in maintaining its original character and offsetting the danger of it becoming a clone town filled with national 'anywhere, any town' chain stores, which are rapidly becoming a feature of other parts of the United Kingdom.

WEST STREET

TWO GENERAL VIEWS of West Street with the Market Cross in the distance. The substantial red-brick building on the left was built in 1904 to accommodate the Oliver Whitby School, which dates back to the eighteenth century. The substantial main entrance is topped by the school crest and further up the school motto, *Vis et Sapientia,* which roughly translates as 'Strength and Wisdom'. As the line of shops are followed in the general direction of the Market Cross, two other

substantial eighteenth-century buildings can be seen, one-time separate hostelries The Dolphin and The Anchor.

LOOKING AT THIS same view today, the first thing to be noted is that the former Oliver Whitby School building has been converted into a department store. With this small amount of information, it also explains why a branch of House of Fraser, a shop that would normally have an unbroken run of plate glass display windows, should possess an incongruous break in the middle of its high-street façade. As for the former Dolphin and Anchor Hotel, so named after amalgamating the two public houses, this had also seen a substantial reduction in the area it once occupied; further shops have intruded into this section of West Street.

MARKET DAY

IT WAS NOT until 1871 that Chichester gained a purpose-built cattle market. Before then, people had to pen their animals within areas set aside in the main streets of the town, especially in East Street as pictured here. The inconvenience to residents can only be imagined, given the amount of animal feed and droppings that would have accumulated by the end of any market day, when as many as 15,000 sheep, oxen, pigs and horses would have been moving around the city. The condition of the streets, as a result of this accumulation of animal filth, also explains why the city, at that time, had high childhood morbidity and mortality rates. Following a petition, delivered to the City Corporation in 1865, serious thought was given to the removal of the market from the centre of the city, with a committee identifying a site close to Eastgate and adjacent to Snag Lane (now Market Avenue). Here, work was taken in clearing the site of some existing buildings, putting down drainage and the construction of a new roadway and walls.

IN MANY RESPECTS, matters have now turned full circle. The livestock market did move to the purpose-built market and it remained there for almost 100 years. However, more recently the market – but not the livestock element of it – has returned to East Street, with a general market held on Wednesday and Saturday mornings until about 3 p.m. (earlier if it's raining) and a separate Farmers' Market on the first and third Friday of each month.

ST PANCRAS' CHURCH

PASSING IN FRONT of St Pancras' church, cattle are being herded to the nearby livestock market sometime around 1960 in this photograph. The building to the left is the Gaumont cinema, which at that time had been recently closed, while St Pancras' church is to the right. Although standing on a medieval site, having originally been built during the fourteenth century or earlier, St Pancras' was destroyed during the Civil War and remained derelict until rebuilt between 1749 and 1750 at a cost £805. Among those who donated to this rebuild were the Countess of Derby and the Duke of Richmond, and the generosity of both was marked by two separate windows at the south end of the

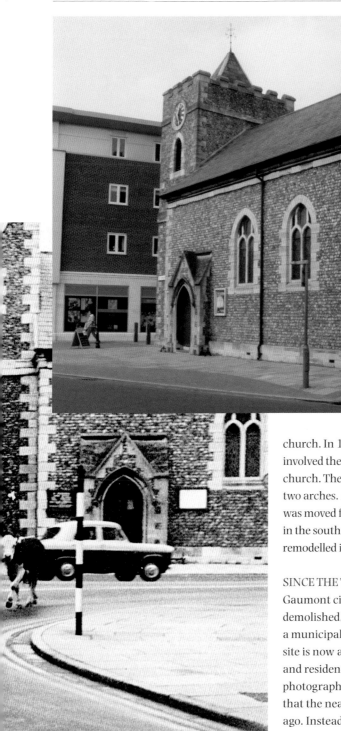

church. In 1869 the north aisle was added, which involved the demolition of the north wall of the church. The north wall was replaced by a pillar and two arches. At the same time the main entrance was moved from the tower to its present position in the south wall and the rest of the church was remodelled in a more Victorian style.

SINCE THE TAKING of the earlier photograph, the Gaumont cinema building has been completely demolished, having first been converted into a municipal swimming pool, and the former site is now a mixed development of shops and residences. A view similar to the earlier photograph would no longer be possible, given that the nearby cattle market closed two decades ago. Instead, the more recent photograph shows St Pancras' church and part of the structure that has replaced the former cinema.

ST MARTIN'S SQUARE

The earlier view shows one of the numerous Georgian period houses that still very much dominate this area of Chichester, with this particular view dating to the 1930s. It is here, also,

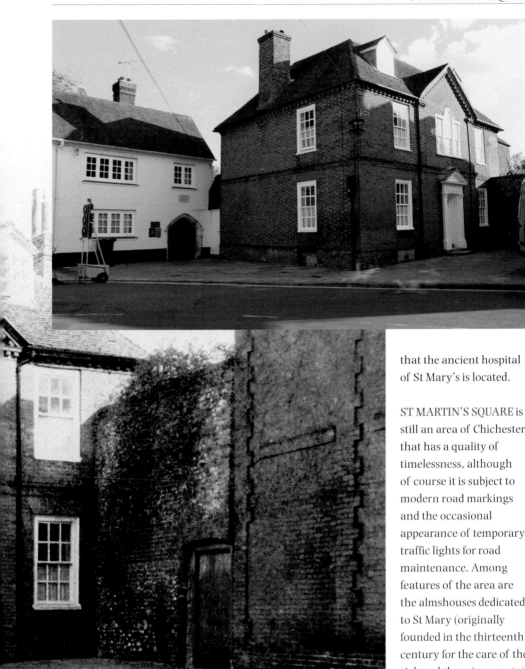

that the ancient hospital of St Mary's is located.

ST MARTIN'S SQUARE is still an area of Chichester that has a quality of timelessness, although of course it is subject to modern road markings and the occasional appearance of temporary traffic lights for road maintenance. Among features of the area are the almshouses dedicated to St Mary (originally founded in the thirteenth century for the care of the sick and those in poverty) and the former site of Chichester's smallest medieval parish church (now converted into a pleasant garden).

EDES HOUSE

EDES HOUSE, ORIGINALLY named Westgate House because of its proximity to the original Roman gate, was completed in 1696. It is one of a series of impressive houses dating to a time when Chichester was becoming increasingly prosperous due to its connections with the corn trade. Edes House is a fine five-bayed two-storey building that was once incorrectly attributed to Christopher Wren and was the one-time family home of John and Hannah Edes. That John Edes was able to finance such a substantial building was a result of his owning lands in Chidham and possibly a malting in Chichester. According to James Spershott, a Baptist minister in eighteenth-century Chichester who wrote his memories of the city, he viewed Westgate as

'the Best house in the City', believing it to have only one drawback, that of it possessing 'transom windows' rather than more fashionable sashes.

ALTHOUGH THE TWO pictures of Edes House are separated by more than fifty years, the changes discernible are very limited. In terms of ownership, however, the house is no longer a private dwelling having been bought by West Sussex County Council in 1916. Initially it served as offices to the council but was superseded in this role upon the building of the present County Hall in 1936. It was then used as the County Library headquarters before conversion in 1967 to provide accommodation for the County and Diocesan Record Offices. With a new County Record Office having been provided in Orchard Street in 1989, the council chose to restore the house for use by the County Council and the community. The total cost of the restoration scheme, including fees and the provision of furniture and equipment, was approximately £1.5 million. Nowadays the house, a Grade I listed building, is used for meetings connected with the business of the County Council during the day and for artistic and cultural activities at other times, while it can also be hired as a venue that can include weddings.

PALLANT HOUSE

PALLANT HOUSE, WITH the earlier photograph dating to the 1960s, is very much of the same period as Edes House, having been completed in 1713. The man behind this project was Henry Peckham; it is usually assumed that Peckham's wealth was garnered from the Portuguese wine trade. Given that Peckham was also an active Tory politician, a political group which at that time was associated with the Jacobite cause, it is interesting that he had the royal coat of arms placed on the keystone of the building. Presumably this was to ensure that in any Jacobite rising against the Hanoverians (and a serious threat to the throne certainly arose in the year after the building was completed), Peckham would not be presumed to be a rebel in the midst of a county that was generally loyal to both the existing monarchy and the Anglican Church. An unusual feature of the building is the peculiar birds that sit astride the gateway piers, leading to the house being sometime referred to as 'Dodo House'.

PALLANT HOUSE NOW serves as an art gallery, a role that it has performed since 1982. Prompting the move in this direction was Walter Hussey, the Dean of Chichester Cathedral who left his personal art collection to the city in 1977 on condition that it should be shown in Pallant House.

At that time the house was owned by the district council, having been used as council offices since 1919. The Hussey collection now forms the basis of a permanent collection that is also supported by temporary exhibitions and a programme of workshops, talks, tours and live performances. The house itself is Grade I listed and prior to its conversion to an art gallery was subject to a full restoration programme that was instigated in 1979. More recently Pallant House has seen the addition of a contemporary adjoining wing that led to a temporary period of closure before its reopening to the public as Pallant House Gallery in 2006. This view emphasises the new wing, which, although in receipt of the Gulbenkian Prize in 2007, is viewed by many Cicestrians as out of keeping in an area that is the heart of Georgian Chichester. Even less pleasing is a rearward extension that overshadows its Georgian neighbours.

THE LIVESTOCK MARKET

FOR MANY CENTURIES Chichester, although possessing an important livestock market, had no special area set aside for the sale of farm animals (see page 38). Instead, it was held in the city streets, resulting in central streets occupied by hundreds of animals brought for sale on each market day. It was a situation that was allowed to continue well into the nineteenth century, with the city fathers ill-prepared to spend money on a purpose-built location. In fact, it became one of the great scandals of the city, with many citizens eventually signing a petition that demanded action on the part of the City Corporation. The outcome was the setting up of a committee that was to recommend a site close to Eastgate. An interesting choice, as this particular land was owned by five members of the council, all of whom readily agreed to sell the land at a price that was much above its then current value. Nevertheless, the sale went through with necessary preparation work for the new market beginning during the early part of 1870 and the market officially opened during the following year. The livestock market finally closed in 1990, with the earlier photograph taken in October 1990, on the eve of its closure. Since then, the site has been used to extend the city's car parking facilities but with occasional use as a farmer's market and for Sunday car-boot sales.

MORE RECENTLY, THE market has returned to the central shopping areas of Chichester. This makes a great deal of sense as it attracts people into the city centre and makes full use of streets that might (through the arrival of the internet and out

of town shopping malls) become empty and lifeless; the market, through the encouragement of small local traders and other similar businesses, will help Chichester survive in its fight against becoming a clone town.

THE
MILITARY
PARADE

WITH A BARRACKS located close to the city centre, Chichester has witnessed a good many military parades over the passing years. During the time of the French and Napoleonic Wars, such parades were particularly common as the area was an important muster point for regiments either defending the south coast or about to be embarked abroad. On this occasion, the parade is slightly different: volunteer members of the 1st Sussex (Chichester) Battalion of the Home Guard march along what appears to be Market Avenue. Recruitment for the Home Guard began in May 1940, allowing those who were otherwise ineligible for military service to

play a role in the defence of the country at a time when invasion threatened. Regular training sessions of the Chichester Home Guard were held in the drill hall located along East Walls, with rifle practice at Funtington and endless patrols throughout the local area.

DESPITE THE CLOSURE of the military barracks, military parades are a continuing feature of Chichester life, with former regiments that were based in the city making an occasional return to affirm those earlier links. The 'Red Caps' or Royal Military Police, who possess the honour of the 'freedom of the city', returned to Chichester for one such parade on 16 June 2011 (Sussex Day) and were addressed by the mayor of the city, Tony French. The link with this regiment goes back to 1964 when Roussillon Barracks became their depot and training establishment.

EASTGATE SQUARE

IT WAS WHILE staying in a house in Eastgate Square that the poet John Keats began to write *The Eve of St Agnes*, a poem which tells the story of young lovers driven apart by feuding families. Always busy, in part because it is a well-used entry point to the city, Eastgate Square has not always been the most attractive end of the city, spoilt by the frequency of traffic that also undermines its value as a shopping area. Nevertheless, Sharp Garland, described as a grocer and provision merchant in the 1920s, survived here for much of the previous century, attracting a clientele from far and wide. The carefully parked delivery van also carries the Sharp Garland name. The premises once occupied by Sharp Garland were demolished in 1964.

MORE RECENTLY ATTEMPTS have been made to revive the fortunes of Eastgate Square through the construction of a mixed development of residential flats and modern retail outlets. Helping create the upmarket feel that Eastgate Square has long been without, there is now a pavement café situated in a more secluded part of the square. In a letter written by Keats in 1819 while staying in Eastgate Square, he wrote to his brother George describing invitations to card parties with 'old dowagers' in the City. One suspects that the equivalence of such a letter would now be an email composed on the tables of this open-air coffee shop.

THE DARK CLOISTER

'A BIT OF Old Chichester' is the original caption of the early photograph, which actually depicts 'the dark cloister', a formerly covered passageway that links Vicar's Close to the cloisters of the cathedral and runs along the south side of the thirteenth-century chapel of St Faith. The photograph was taken sometime before the First World War. In some respects 'the dark cloister' passageway has similarities to the Crooked S, another narrow lane but one that connects North Street with St Martins and was once called The Shambles. This gives a considerable clue as to what the Crooked 'S' was like in earlier times, for although it once contained entrances

to a number of tiny houses, the word 'Shambles' is an obsolete term for an open-air slaughterhouse. In other cities, such as York and Stroud, this was where the butcheries were to be found. In Chichester the Crooked 'S' under its former title served a similar purpose and would have been lined with slaughterhouses.

RETURNING TO 'THE dark cloister', while still recognizable, a number of changes are discernible, not least of which is the insertion of modern windows to the building on the left (the Chapel of St Faith) and the partial removal of an overhanging building at the eastern end. At one time a number of similar buildings lined the passageway, which led to it being known as 'the dark cloister'.

EAST STREET

BATHED IN BRIGHT sunlight, hundreds of Cicestrians patiently await the arrival of King Edward VII on 30 July 1904. The lining of the street with flags and bunting was typical of how the city celebrated numerous royal events and national occasions. Royalty made a number of visits to the city during the early twentieth century, with Edward VII returning to the city in 1908 and visiting the thirteenth-century St Mary's Hospital, when he met some of the patients. It was the turn of George V to visit the city in August 1913. On this latter occasion he bestowed the title 'Royal' upon the West Sussex Hospital. Looking at East Street on the occasion of this depicted royal visit are the

premises at the very beginning of this street, the Market Cross being just behind the camera. On the right, and just creeping into view, is the London City and Midland Bank (No. 94) and immediately next door is Lipton Ltd (No. 93), a branch of a national chain of grocers. The shop with the bow window on the right (No. 92) was, and remained for many years, a wine merchant and later the Royal Arms public house.

THE MODERN-DAY photograph is a general view of East Street looking in a westerly direction with the Cross immediately behind. A dress shop now occupies the former site of the Royal Arms but many of the other buildings along this side have been replaced since the earlier photograph. The north side of East Street has also seen a great deal of rebuilding with many of the earlier shops also completely replaced, although the distinctive late-Victorian bank complex (now NatWest) still continues to serve this riole. Finally, of course, much of East Street is now pedestrianized, making shopping in this area both considerably less hazardous and a generally much more enjoyable experience.

SOUTHGATE

A VIEW OF Southgate from the footbridge looking east and dating to 1951. The building on the left is the former police station that was built in 1857 to house a newly formed rural constabulary. In later years, due to the merging of both the city and rural constabularies, this also became the station responsible for matters both inside and outside the city area. During the late-1930s a new police station was built in Kingsham Road, making this building redundant. Eventually it

was demolished, making way for an extension to the bus station. The railway line itself was first opened on 8 June 1846, then the London, Brighton and South Coast Railway (LBSCR) that created a link, via Ford, to Brighton. Soon after, continuing work on

the line saw the opening of the westward running section that connected first to Havant in March 1847 and eventually Portsmouth in June 1847.

IN THIS SIMILAR view, taken in 2011, an electrically powered train that has come from the Brighton direction is about to enter Chichester station. The former police station is no longer to be seen, this having been replaced by a brick extension to the rear of the bus station that houses a café and retail stores. The automatic barriers, which are raised to allow traffic through, are another new feature. Heavier gated structures, which were opened and closed manually rather than mechanically, can be seen in the earlier picture. The length of time these barriers are left in the downward position is highly contentious, often creating long tailbacks of irritated motorists.

THE HORNET

THIS VIEW OF the Hornet shows the carriage business of John Grist, whose premises were at one time situated at the western extreme of the Hornet (No. 3). As a carriage business, John Grist was very important to Chichester, being much like a modern-day garage in that it carried out necessary repairs on horse-drawn carriages and provided reins and other necessary paraphernalia. An additional aspect of the business was that of hiring out carriages, these either self-drive or with a driver.

THE FORMER PREMISES of John Grist have long been swept away, with the site seemingly covered by the premises of the present-day *Chichester Observer* office. In fact, there is no No. 3 in the Hornet as the numbering now starts at 8, signifying that the part of the roadway where John Grist was once to be found has now been reduced in length to provide greater space for traffic. Another significant change is that of the Hornet being part of a gyratory road complex designed to speed traffic into and out of Chichester. While motorists thereby gain, the loss must surely be to local residents who, in visiting a number of small and diverse retail outlets, have themselves to contend with this speeding traffic.

CANAL BASIN
AND CUT

TOWARDS THE END of the wars with Napoleon,
work began on a waterway that would connect
Portsmouth with London. In part, the new route
was achieved through the construction of the
Portsmouth-Arun Canal but use was also made
of existing navigable waters such as those of
Chichester Harbour and the Arun and Wey rivers.
The city of Chichester was not forgotten: a canal
basin and cut began to be constructed in 1818,
with the latter running to Chichester Harbour
at Birdham where it connected to the new route
running between London and Portsmouth. For
merchants of Chichester this proved an undoubted
advantage, allowing heavy cargoes of coal and
building materials to be brought to the very centre
of the city. Given that Chichester at this time was
in the midst of economic depression, the work of

building the new cut and basin helped reduce local unemployment, with those on poor relief being used to cut sections of the canal.

WHILE THE EARLIER picture shows the canal as it appeared on a cold winter's morning in December 1935, the latter shows a similar stretch during the summer of 2011. The cut very much adds to the attractions of the city, providing quiet waterside walks with sudden surprise views of the distant cathedral spire. For those less inclined to walk, or simply wishing to enjoy a restful afternoon, a visit to the Canal Trust shop at the basin can secure a boat trip or the hiring of a rowing boat. The canal has sections bounded by mature trees and also travels through open farmland with good views of the South Downs. The tow path is a designated public footpath and can also be used by cyclists.

63

PRIORY PARK

IN THE MIDST of Priory Park is the choir of a medieval church that was built by the Franciscan monks, known as the Greyfriars, during the late-thirteenth century as part of a friary that they had founded in the city. Following the Reformation and the suppression of the friary, the City Corporation acquired the site and buildings in 1541. While much of the friary was subsequently demolished, the choir of the church was converted into a Guildhall. Probably completed as the choir of the church in 1282, it comprises five and a half bays, and in its eastern wall it has a

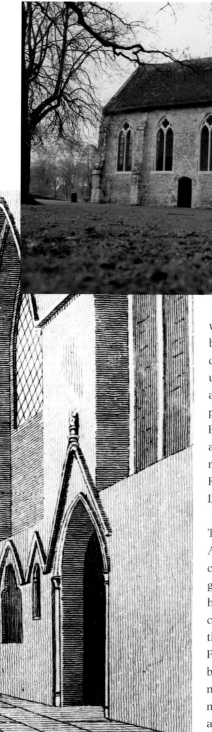

window of five tall lancets divided by slender shafts. Two blocked doorways on the north side probably led to the cloisters, while the chancel arch is blocked. A further use of the building was that of the Shire Hall for assizes and for election purposes up until 1888. Here, in 1808, a particularly famous trial took place when the poet William Blake was tried on a charge of sedition and subsequently acquitted. The park itself became a subscribers' park in the mid-nineteenth century when it was owned by the Duke of Richmond, but it was presented to the city council by the Duke in 1918.

THE PARK IS now managed by Chichester District Council. A quiet corner of Chichester, the park regularly hosts cricket matches in summer and has a splendid bowling green, a children's play area and an aviary. The park has been used on many occasions for large community celebrations at Coronations and Jubilees, as well as being the focus of the Chichester Gala and the Real Ale and Jazz Festival. Apart from the former Guildhall, a grade I listed building, Priory Park contains two further scheduled monuments: the City Walls and the remains of a Norman motte. Little, unfortunately, is made of the latter, which is an area of the park that usually lacks the care and attention it clearly deserves.

ROYAL WEST SUSSEX HOSPITAL

LOCATED IN THE Broyle, the West Sussex Hospital is seen in this engraving shortly after its completion in 1826. It was not until 1913 that it received the title 'Royal' following a visit to the hospital by King George V. With an original construction cost of £8,985, the building of the hospital was financed through a subscription scheme of which Charles Lennox, the 5th Duke of

Richmond, was the largest single subscriber. The foundation stone was laid on 10 June 1825, and after taking just over a year to complete, the new building was ready for occupation on 31 October 1826. At that time the hospital offered bed space for approximately fifty patients.

HAVING BECOME PART of the National Health Service in 1948, the Royal West Sussex Hospital saw continued development that included a new chapel and a casualty department. However, by 1970 the 'Royal West' was faced with great expense to upgrade its fire precautions and, as a result, patients were all transferred to St Richard's Hospital, with the last hutted ward closed in 1990. Finally the building was put up for sale in March 1994 and subsequently converted into apartments, as this picture shows. This particular building was once the nurses' home, and each window represents a bedroom that led off a central corridor. Incidentally, the wisteria, because of its great age, is subject to a preservation order.

CHARITY COLLECTORS

THESE EARLY COLLECTORS for charity are collecting money for the Chichester Infirmary. In reality this was the West Sussex Hospital (renamed Royal West Sussex Hospital in 1913), which at that time, and to use its full name, was known as the West Sussex, East Hampshire and Chichester General Infirmary and Dispensary

(the charity collectors had chosen to shorten the name). At that time (the photograph probably dates to around 1905) there was no National Health Service and hospitals were entirely dependent on charitable or private means to ensure they could serve the needs of the less affluent.

LESS OF A charity but more of a helping hand is *The Big Issue*, which was set up in 1991 to provide homeless and vulnerably housed people with an opportunity to earn a legitimate income. Independent vendors are to be seen regularly in Chichester, identifiable by a photo ID and a distinctive jacket, proof of the seller not only having received training but also having signed an agreed code of conduct. On this occasion, *The Big Issue* vendor is seen in East Street, just outside the NatWest Bank, this in itself an interesting contrast. In common with High street shopping centres in many other towns, the main shopping streets of Chichester have also gained, over the years, several charity shops, these often selling some incredible bargains. Again, this is a very different approach to the hospital flag days and collecting boxes that was frequently the main approach taken by charitable organisations in earlier times.

GRAYLINGWELL

DURING THE FIRST World War Graylingwell Hospital, built originally as a Victorian lunatic asylum, was given over to the military for the purpose of nursing those wounded on the Western Front. Here are to be seen members of the Royal Army Medical Corps who served at the hospital during this period. Many of the original doctors and nurses had remained at the hospital following the transfer of civilian patients to other parts of the country, with Dr Kidd, the medical superintendent of the pre-war hospital, given the rank of lieutenant-general. Providing assistance to an over-stretched staff during this period were local volunteers often drawn from the Red Cross and St John's Ambulance Brigade as well as local boy scouts, the latter serving as messengers. On return to civilian use, plans were introduced for further buildings to provide an admission hospital (Summersdale), nurses'

home (Pinewood), a block for female tuberculosis patients, a female convalescent villa and a villa for female working patients (Richmond and Kingsmead). Construction began in 1930 and the new structures, designed to complement the existing building, were opened in 1933. Graylingwell hospital was passed to the National Health Service in 1948, by which time its in-patient capacity had exceeded 1,000.

GRAYLINGWELL HOSPITAL OFFICIALLY closed in 2003, although part of the site remained in partial health use, with services still operating from the admission hospital, Barnfield house and new buildings located close to the south lodge gate. The nurses' home has also been retained temporarily for accommodation for the local district general hospital. House building on land to the south of the site has recently been extended to incorporate part of the grounds, and a new access road has led to the demolition of the former female villas. The surrounding open land is currently used by the public and adjacent university for sports and recreational facilities. It was also this same land, prior to its purchase for construction of the hospital, and then Graylingwell Farm, that had once been home to Anna Sewell, the author of *Black Beauty*.

THE SHIPPAM'S
EAST WALLS FACTORY

HERE, IN 1911, work is underway on constructing the Shippam's East Walls factory that was to become one of Chichester's major landmarks. Upon its completion, food processing was undertaken, an operation that made the company a household name throughout the length and breadth of the British Isles. It was here that the distinctly shaped vacuum-sealed glass jars were filled with potted meat and fish before transfer to the local railway station for distribution around the world. So famed was the product that, in 1924, the factory received a royal visit from Queen Mary, the consort of George V, who expressed considerable interest in both the conditions of

work and the product of this factory. Shippam's was a family-run business that had connections with Chichester going back to the very inception of the company when Shipston Shippam opened a shop in the city in 1750.

ALTHOUGH THE ORIGINAL shell of the Shippam's East Walls factory still remains, it is no longer used for the manufacturing and processing of foods. In 2002, by which time Shippam's was part of an international conglomerate, a decision was taken to close the factory and centre food processing upon a new site that was situated in Terminus Road and formerly owned by Uniq. Here a patchwork of buildings existed that had once been used to make yoghurts and desserts. Part of the original structure was kept but over 80 per cent was demolished and £15 million spent on its redevelopment. With a workforce of nearly 200, the new Terminus Road site (Unit 12) produces ambient sauces, spreadables, ready meals in bottles, jars, cans, plastic pots and flexible pouches. As for the East Walls factory site, following its sale it has been redeveloped, with part of the original façade along East Walls retained but with the production building (located to the east side of Chichester's main shopping centre) and former social club (located on the opposite side of East Walls road) both demolished.

ROUSSILLON BARRACKS

THE BARRACKS ALONGSIDE Broyle Road can date their origin to 1795 when construction of a small block was begun. The passing years saw considerable enlargement, although they were clearly not quite fit for purpose upon the outbreak of the First World War, when particular demand was placed on them. At that time, a new recruit to the Royal Sussex Regiment vented his complaints in a letter he wrote to his mother: 'The barracks [at Chichester] are old-fashioned, consisting of a large enclosed space with numerous erections built bungalow style sufficient for the comfortable accommodation of 500 men. In all there were about 1,200 in the barracks on the day of our arrival, all raw recruits. There were only about six NCO's to take charge of the whole lot. Needless to say the place was in a hopeless confusion.' As for it having acquired the name Roussillon, this was not until 1958. The name Roussillon was taken from the Royal Roussillon Regiment of France, which was overwhelmed by the 35th Regiment at Quebec in 1759 and whose white plume was later incorporated in the badge of the Royal Sussex Regiment.

IN 2008, FOLLOWING a determination that the barracks were no longer to be retained by
the army, the site was sold to English Partnerships to 'ease the obvious shortage of supply of
affordable housing stock in the local area'. Only the keep remains in the hands of the army, this
being retained as a recruitment office. In March 2011 planning permission was granted for a
252 home redevelopment of the former site, with demolition work beginning later that same
year. At that time, completion of fifty homes, located in the north-west corner of the site, was
anticipated for spring 2012. A major concern, given the extensive nature of the development, is
the infrastructure of the area and whether existing roads can take such a potential increase in
likely usage, although efforts to reduce dependence on the private car will be lessened by facilities
to be put in place to encourage walking and cycling, the provision of public transport, and a car
club for residents.

ORLITS ESTATE

HOUSES ON THE Orlits estate were built as a result of the earlier post-war housing crisis. The unusual name of the estate comes from the employment of a particular housing design produced by the Orlits Company based in Scotland. At the end of the Second World War there was a pressing need for more housing to be built as rapidly as possible. To facilitate this, the Orlits Company had adopted the use of houses designed by Erwin Katona, a citizen of Czechoslovakia who had relocated to the United Kingdom in 1938. A fundamental of the design was employment of prefabricated building materials to ensure rapid construction. The foundations having been dug, these were used to support pre-cast concrete columns at fixed intervals that were faced externally with large high-sided concrete slabs. Internally, and providing wall partitions, breeze blocks finished in plaster were utilized. A further

factor associated with the Orlits Estate was that much of the construction work, together with two other post-war estates, Whyke and Parklands, was undertaken by German prisoners of war.

DUE TO BOTH the speed of construction and the quality of production, over time the pre-reinforced concrete used in the Orlits Estate began to deteriorate, particularly at construction joints and junctions between components, with a gradual reduction in structural effectiveness. This resulted in houses built to the Orlits design being designated as defective under the Housing Defects Act 1984. For Chichester this led to an early replacement of houses on the estate. This more recent photograph looks across the Green but shows only houses of a much more recent design. During the earlier phase of replacing the original post-war prefabs, those living in these houses were provided with more traditionally designed brick and mortar houses built on the outskirts of the estate, so allowing the houses from which they had vacated to be demolished and replaced with other more durable homes.

SLOE FAIR

THE CHICHESTER SLOE Fair is an annual event held on 20 October each year (or Monday 21 October, to avoid Sundays) since the reign of Henry I (1100-35). Its unusual name relates to the one-time existence of a sloe tree in a field near Northgate where the fair is traditionally held. Coldness and rain always accompanied the fair, so wellingtons and warm clothes were essential.

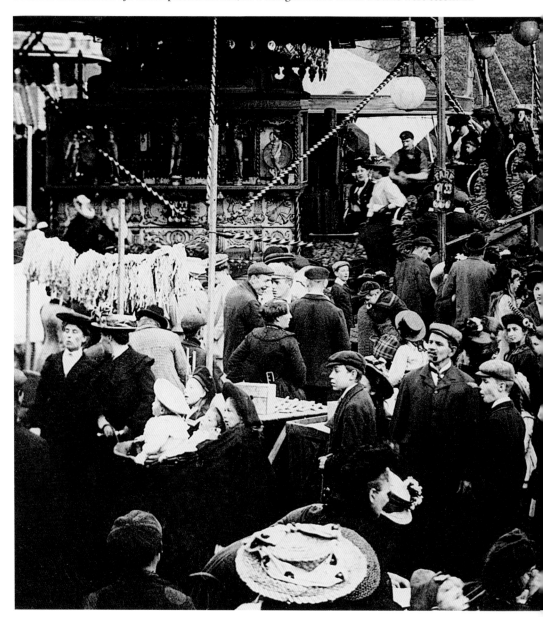

THAT, OF COURSE, has now
changed: the site of the fair
is now a tarmacked car park
and global warming ensures
occasional summer-time
temperatures. Despite attempts
in the past to kill the fair, it is a
definite survivor and was only
abandoned during the wartime
years of 1939 to 1945, when
a van was parked on the field
on each 20 October to ensure
that a break in the continuance
of the fair would not be used
as an excuse to abolish it. The
two pictures are something of
a contrast, one showing the
fair at the beginning of the
twentieth century with one of
the more exciting rides of the
period compared with a white
knuckle Sloe Fair ride of the
early twenty-first century.

A COSY TEA ROOM

THE 1920S WAS an age where a day out at the shops would often conclude with a visit to a favourite tea shop for an afternoon 'cuppa'. Where shopping centres today are dominated by fast food outlets and coffee venues, this was not the case in Chichester in an age where self-service had yet to be invented. This is an interior view of T.H. Fuller & Son, whose premises formerly stood on the corner of East Street and St Martin's Lane. T.H. Fuller & Son proclaimed themselves 'a high class bakers' with one simple motto: 'quality'. Here uniformed waitresses provided 'hot and cold luncheons and dainty teas'. As times changed, and middle-class pretentiousness gave way to a less class-conscious post-war world, the same site became 'Akers the Bakers'.

NOWADAYS, THE SITE formerly occupied by T.H. Fuller & Son is home to Clinton Cards, while on the far side of St Martin's Lane is the Marks & Spencer food outlet, decked out in its Christmas 2011 colours and patterns. Tea shops are now few and far between in Chichester, having been replaced by coffee store chains and fast food outlets. On the other hand, the city does have a good selection of restaurants, many offering culinary dishes from across the world. So you gain some and you lose some!

THE UNIVERSITY

CHICHESTER UNIVERSITY BEGAN life as the Bishop Otter Memorial Training College for Schoolmasters and was established by the Anglican Church to commemorate a former bishop of Chichester who had devoted much of his life to bringing about improvements in education. Initially, the new College was to be found in St Martin's Lane before moving to dedicated premises in College Lane. At that time it had no certain future, the number of students coming forward to enrol being lower than hoped. Eventually, however, it was to find a particular niche that was to

ensure its survival when it was decided to abandon the training of future schoolmasters for that of schoolmistresses.

TODAY THESE SAME buildings, combined with a number of more recent additions, including a new Learning Resources Centre and a Sports Activity and Research Centre, still serve the needs of education. No longer a college but now a university, the training of teachers is still undertaken but on the Bognor Regis campus that had been originally created in 1946 under the aegis of Bognor Regis College. In 1977 both the Bishop Otter College and that at Bognor Regis were merged, forming the West Sussex Institute of Higher Education. From 1995, the former Bishop Otter College was known as the Chichester Institute of Higher Education. Four years later it gained the power of awarding degrees and became known as University College Chichester before being recognised as a full university in October 2005.

RAILWAY STATION

A VIEW OF Chichester railway station showing the original booking office that was first constructed during the mid-nineteenth century, at the time of the original opening of the railway line. In those early years of Chichester being served by a rail line, the city enjoyed a service that saw eight daily trains running to Brighton and a further eight return trains running to Portsmouth. The journey time varied according to the number of stops involved, with a

journey to Brighton taking a possible one hour and fifteen minutes. Connections could also be made with trains to London but initially this was only possible by journeying through Brighton, the connection via Havant not being possible until 1859 when the line via Havant and Guildford was completed.

THE CURRENT BOOKING office at Chichester is located in the exact same position as that of its predecessor and came about as a result of a general rebuilding of the station that took place in the 1960s. At that time a number of general improvements were made to the platforms, and cycle racks and a new taxi stand were subsequently added. Since 1938, the line has been electrified at a cost of £2.75 million, while the frequency of trains has greatly increased, with five departures an hour in each direction during weekday off-peak periods. A nighttime shot, the station forecourt is one of the best places in Chichester to procure a 'black cab'. This seemed to be less so in the 1950s, when the earlier view was taken.

CHICHESTER MUSEUM

AFTER MANY YEARS of being without a permanent museum, the site of a former corn mill was acquired in Little London and opened as a museum by the Duchess of Albemarle in April 1964. At that time, being in the ownership of the Chichester City Council, it centred much more on the immediate area of Chichester. However, as a result of local government reorganisation, it became a district museum in 1974 with a resulting widened brief of interest. The building itself is of historic interest and clearly added to the nature of the task being undertaken. A much greater failure was

that of the district council to give adequate prominence to the institution, not even able to provide sufficient signage that would alert visitors to its existence.

IN JANUARY 2009, planning permission was given for the construction of a new museum in Tower Street, immediately opposite the library. A definite plus factor for the new building is that it will overlay the site of the Roman baths, so permitting these to be uncovered and visible within the building through a long window facing the street. Less commendable are some of the aspects of the building that include the overall height of its tower, which is out of keeping with other nearby buildings, and the overuse of cladding, which is rather unexciting for a city flagship building. Certainly, the design has been subject to much local criticism, and at the time of it being planned, one local resident said that it would be no less than 'a big featureless block which will degrade the Edwardian buildings around it'. Although not complete by the time this particular photograph was taken, it does permit an assessment to be made as to the architectural merit of the new museum, which is to be named Novium.

THE LOCAL BUS

FULLY LADEN OPEN-top buses carrying staff from Shippam's on their annual outing are about to set out from East Walls. Given that the East Walls factory was still under construction when this photograph was captured, it is fairly easy to give the photograph a date, which must be sometime around 1911. In future years the company would hire similar open-top buses for staff outings but these would be supplied by Southdown Motor Services. However, at the time of the photograph, the Southdown Company, which was created in 1915, had yet to be formed. Following its formation, the Southdown Company soon dominated bus routes throughout Chichester, and its green livery and gold-emblazoned name on the sides of its buses are still fondly remembered. Hopefully, the

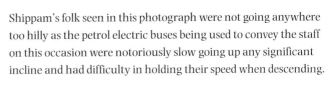

Shippam's folk seen in this photograph were not going anywhere too hilly as the petrol electric buses being used to convey the staff on this occasion were notoriously slow going up any significant incline and had difficulty in holding their speed when descending.

IN CONTRAST TO the struggling petrol electric buses seen leaving East Walls is this modern-day counterpart, a Scania OmniDekka operated by Stagecoach for Chichester University and seen passing along Avenue de Chartres. Why no more green-liveried Southdown buses? Well, in 1985 Southdown had become part of the National Bus Company before being acquired four years later by the Stagecoach Group, with the original green livery eventually replaced by the white and stripes of the owning company. As for this particular bus, clearly operating on behalf of Chichester University, it carries both students and staff between campuses and is part of the university's declared aim of promoting the use of sustainable forms of transport.

GLORIOUS GOODWOOD

THIS NINETEENTH-CENTURY engraving depicts horses and riders preparing for a race at Goodwood. Although racing had been a regular feature of Goodwood for a number of years, the first official meet was not until 1801. The impressive stand, providing a focal point for racing events, was added in 1804. It was the 3rd Duke of Richmond who had first introduced horseracing to Goodwood to provide entertainment for the officers of the Sussex Militia of which he was, at that time, a colonel.

THE POPULARITY OF Goodwood as a racing venue is indisputable, with the racing fraternity regularly passing through Chichester for the twenty or more meetings held each year. Undoubtedly the 'Glorious Goodwood' meeting held in

E.W. 1 - 2 - 3 $\frac{1}{5}$ ODDS

REMEMBER A BAD DAY AT THE RACES IS BETTER THAN A GOOD DAY AT WORK

late July, with its Ladies' Day always on the last Thursday of the month, is the jewel in the crown. Here dress code takes on a particular significance: jackets and ties, cravats or polo-neck sweaters are always a requirement for 'gentlemen' entering the up-market Richmond enclosure, while ladies are expected to dress smartly and encouraged to wear hats at the festival meetings. During the five days of 'Glorious Goodwood', over 100,000 people come to the course, with most undoubtedly sharing the motto of one regular attending bookie to that week of racing, that 'a bad day at the races is better than a good day at work'. But then a bookie would say that... wouldn't he?

PORTSMOUTH WATER

THE ORIGINAL FISHBOURNE waterworks engine house as seen in the 1920s. A major problem for Chichester during the nineteenth century was that of providing a satisfactory supply of uncontaminated drinking water to all its residents. An outbreak of typhoid in 1879 was particularly responsible for highlighting the issue, a total of sixty cases occurring on the western side of the city. Careful enquiries revealed that milk delivered by a local dairy had been contaminated by water drawn from either a nearby well (sited close to a cess pool) or the River Lavant (which had acquired a wide range of unhygienic uses). This underlined and provided further support for the speeding up of efforts that were already in hand for extending the domestic supply of water from the recently constructed waterworks at Fishbourne, then owned by Chichester Waterworks Company but acquired by the City Corporation in 1897.

THE ORIGINAL FACILITY at Fishbourne still serves as a water supply and water treatment works for the Chichester area. However, the earlier buildings have all been demolished and replaced by modern and somewhat austere structures that lack the additional ornamentation that was so favoured by engineers of the Victorian era. Of the buildings to be seen in the modern-day view, the one in the foreground is an engine house for the pumping of water.

THE RURAL SCENE

AN EIGHTEENTH-CENTURY view of the countryside near Chichester, an area that Daniel Defoe, writing in the 1720s, described as 'the most pleasant beautiful country in England'. At this time both farming and husbandry were the primary means of employment in the area around the city with the Chichester markets of absolute importance for the sale of such produce. Every week regular markets for the sale of livestock and locally grown foods were held, with the poorer

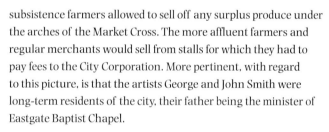

subsistence farmers allowed to sell off any surplus produce under the arches of the Market Cross. The more affluent farmers and regular merchants would sell from stalls for which they had to pay fees to the City Corporation. More pertinent, with regard to this picture, is that the artists George and John Smith were long-term residents of the city, their father being the minister of Eastgate Baptist Chapel.

WHILE THE PRECISE location of the earlier view is uncertain, this modern view of the countryside near Chichester is of West Ashling. The building to be seen is a former mill that stands in front of a mill pond. In using this photograph, two purposes are intended. First and foremost, a reminder that the countryside around Chichester still merits the accolade of being 'the most pleasant beautiful country in England'. The second is as a demonstration of the former wealth of the area having once been generated from land that could produce some of the finest wheat found anywhere in the country. Once harvested, the wheat produced needed to be milled, with a great number of water-powered mills (although the West Ashling mill could also use wind power with the addition of a stationary steam engine that could also drive the millstones as a final option) to be found in the countryside around Chichester.

Other titles published by The History Press

Haunted Chichester

ARRON WEEDALL

This collection of spooky stories contains new and well-known tales from Chichester and the surrounding area. From the sighting of a ghostly armoured soldier seen around Charlton Forest riding a grey horse, to the ghost lady who wears a wide-brimmed hat and flowing dress dating from the late eighteenth century at Bognor's Hotham Park, this well-researched book will appeal to anyone interested in the dark history of the area.

978 0 7524 4554 0

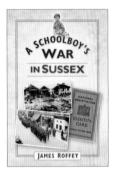

A Schoolboy's War in Sussex

JAMES ROFFEY

Although only children at the time, the Second World War had a permanent effect on the schoolboys who lived through the conflict. Watching a country preparing for war and then being immersed in the horrors of the Blitz brought encounters and events that some will never forget. Now in their seventies and eighties, many are revisiting their memories of this period for the first time. West Sussex was a dangerous place in the wartime years, and this poignant book documents events indelibly inscribed on a generation's minds.

978 0 7524 5518 1

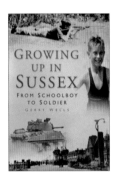

Growing Up In Sussex: From Schoolboy to Soldier

GERRY WELLS

This compelling memoir starts with a boy's journey through the early years of the 1930s: days of the rag and bone man, street lamplighters, Hercule Poirot, and in the background, Hitler. In this nostalgic book, evoking recollections of childhood and wartime in Sussex, the memories are the author's. However, the sights and events are those that will be remembered by many others, and readers will warm to the narrator, who has found the perfect balance of humour and sensitivity.

978 0 7524 4967 8

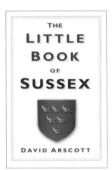

The Little Book of Sussex

DAVID ARSCOTT

A funny, fast-paced, fact-packed compendium of the sort of frivolous, fantastic or simply strange information which no one will want to be without. Here we find out about the most unusual crimes and punishments, eccentric inhabitants, famous sons and daughters and literally hundreds of wacky facts (plus some authentically bizarre bits of historic trivia). David Arscott's new book gathers together a myriad of data on Sussex. There are lots of factual chapters but also plenty of frivolous details which will amuse and surprise.

978 0 7524 5871 7

Visit our website and discover thousands of other History Press books.

www.thehistorypress.co.uk